West Ham Un
Quiz Book

101 Questions That Will Test Your Knowledge Of This Great Football Club

By Chris Carpenter

West Ham United Quiz

This book contains one hundred and one informative and entertaining trivia questions with multiple-choice answers. With 101 questions, some easy, some more challenging, this entertaining book will test your knowledge and memory of the club's long history. You will be asked many questions on a wide range of topics associated with West Ham United Football Club for you to test yourself.

You will be quizzed on players, legends, managers, opponents, transfer deals, trophies, records, honours, fixtures, terrace songs and much more, guaranteeing you both an educational experience and hours of fun. Educational, enjoyable and fun, the West Ham Quiz Book will provide lots of entertainment for Hammers fans of all ages and will prove you know your Hammers trivia in this fun addictive quiz book.

2024/25 Season Edition

FOREWORD

When I was asked to write a foreword to this book I was flattered.

I have known the author Chris Carpenter for a number of years and his knowledge of facts and figures is phenomenal.

His love for football and his skill in writing quiz books make him the ideal man to pay homage to my great love West Ham United Football Club.

This book came about as a result of a challenge on a golf course.

I do hope you enjoy the book.

Craig Simpson

Let's start with some relatively easy questions.

1. When were West Ham United founded?
   - A. 1875
   - B. 1885
   - C. 1895

2. What is West Ham United's nickname?
   - A. The Anvils
   - B. The Hammers
   - C. The Spanners

3. Who has made the most appearances for the club in total?
   - A. Billy Bonds
   - B. Frank Lampard Senior
   - C. Bobby Moore

4. Who has made the most *League* appearances for the club?
   - A. Billy Bonds
   - B. Trevor Brooking
   - C. Bobby Moore

5. Who is the club's record goal scorer?
   - A. John Dick
   - B. Geoff Hurst
   - C. Vic Watson

6. Who has scored the most penalties for the club?
   - A. Julian Dicks
   - B. Mark Noble

C. Ray Stewart

7. Who is the fastest ever goal scorer for the club?
    A. Ken Bainbridge
    B. Tony Cottee
    C. Stewart Downing

8. Who or what is the club mascot?
    A. Claret the Lion
    B. Hammerhead
    C. Herbie The Hammer

9. What is the highest number of goals that West Ham United has scored in a league season?
    A. 99
    B. 100
    C. 101

10. What is the fewest number of goals that West Ham United has conceded in a league season?
    A. 28
    B. 29
    C. 30

OK, so here are the answers to the first ten questions. If you get seven or more right, you are on track, but don't get too cocky, as the questions do get harder.

A1. The earliest generally accepted incarnation of West Ham United was founded in 1895 as the Thames Ironworks team in June 1895. Following disputes over the running of the club, Thames Ironworks FC was disbanded in June 1900, and then re-launched as West Ham United FC on 5th July 1900.

A2. Famously the club are known as "The Hammers" thanks to their original roots as a "works team" in the ironwork trade. The club is also fondly referred to as "The Irons" in some circles, and also "The Academy of Football" in recognition of the club coaching young talent and the style of football associated with the club.

A3. Synonymous with the club for over twenty years, Billy Bonds holds the appearance record with an incredible 804 in total.

A4. It's that man again. Billy Bonds holds the League appearances record, racking up 663 games in total.

A5. Vic Watson smashed in an amazing 326 goals for West Ham in his time at the club between 1920 and 1935.

A6. Miles ahead of the competition, Ray Stewart scored 78 penalties for the club. He played for the club between 1979 and 1991 and became a favourite with the fans who nicknamed him "Tonka" after Tonka Toys, which were described as 'indestructible'.

A7. Ken Bainbridge holds the fastest goal scored after kick of record, scoring after just 9 seconds in a game against Barnsley on 29th August 1949.

A8. West Ham unveiled Hammerhead as the club's mascot to a mixed reception in 2011, replacing Bubbles the Bear. Hammerhead has grown to become a popular mascot at the club, and is always happy to have his picture taken with young fans.

A9. West Ham scored a record 101 goals back in Division Two in the 1957/58 season.

A10. The Hammers had one of the meanest defences around in the 1980/81 season, conceding a miserly 29 goals.

OK, let's have some ground related questions.

11. Where does West Ham United play their home games?
    A. Boleyn Stadium
    B. London Stadium
    C. Queen Elizabeth Stadium

12. What is the stadium's capacity?
    A. 60,000
    B. 62,500
    C. 66,000

13. Who was the first match in the new stadium against?
    A. Astra Giurgiu
    B. NK Domzale
    C. Juventus

14. Who did the club play in their first League game at the new stadium?
    A. Arsenal
    B. Bournemouth
    C. Watford

15. What is the size of the pitch?
    A. 105x60 yards
    B. 112x72 yards
    C. 115x75 yards

16. What was the club's old ground called?
    A. Blundell Park

B. Boundary Park

C. Upton Park

17. What is the club's record attendance at the old ground?
    A. 41,322
    B. 42,322
    C. 43,322

18. What is the club's record attendance at the new stadium?
    A. 58,751
    B. 60,988
    C. 62,449

19. What song do the players run out to?
    A. Hammer Time
    B. I'm Forever Blowing Bubbles
    C. Iron Man

20. Who was the first band to play a concert at the new stadium?
    A. AC/DC
    B. Guns 'N Roses
    C. The Rolling Stones

Here are the answers to the last set of questions.

A11. West Ham plays their home games at the London Stadium, the former 2012 Olympics Stadium, which was reconfigured to accommodate the Hammers.

A12. Although the stadium has 66,000 seats, its capacity is reduced for football matches under the terms of the lease. As from the beginning of the 2023/24 season its capacity for football matches is 62,500.

A13. The official opening match was a friendly against Juventus on 7th August 2016, but the first game played by the club at the new stadium was a Europa League game against NK Domzale three days earlier on 4th August 2016.

A14. The first league game at the new stadium was against AFC Bournemouth on 21st August 2016, with West Ham winning 1-0.

A15. With an area of 115 yards long and 75 yards wide, the pitch has plenty of space to accommodate an expressive, expansive style of football.

A16. West Ham used to play their home games at the historic Boleyn Ground, Upton Park in East London.

A17. 42,322 fans squeezed into the ground on 17th October 1970 to see the Hammers play local rivals Tottenham Hotspur in Division One (old) match. This was in the days when the North and South Banks were terraced, as was the old 'Chicken Run' to the front of the East Stand.

A18. According to Wikipedia the official record attendance at the new stadium was against Brighton on 21st August 2022 – an official attendance figure of 62,449.

A19. If you don't know this, you should probably stop reading now. It is of course 'I'm Forever Blowing Bubbles'.

A20. On 4th June 2016 AC/DC became the first band to play a concert at the stadium since its redevelopment following the 2012 Olympics

Now we move onto some questions about the club's records.

21. What is the club's record win in any competition?
    A. 8-0
    B. 9-0
    C. 10-0

22. Who did they beat?
    A. Blackburn Rovers
    B. Bolton Wanderers
    C. Bury

23. In which season?
    A. 1973/74
    B. 1983/84
    C. 1993/94

24. What is the club's record win in the league?
    A. 8-0
    B. 9-0
    C. 10-0

25. Who did they beat?
    A. Stockport County
    B. Sunderland
    C. Swansea City

26. In which season?
    A. 1957/58
    B. 1963/64
    C. 1968/69

27. What is the club's record defeat?
   A. 0-7
   B. 0-8
   C. 0-9

28. Who against?
   A. Sheffield United
   B. Sheffield Wednesday
   C. Sunderland

29. What is the club's record win in the Premier League?
   A. 4-0
   B. 5-0
   C. 6-0

30. Who has scored the most hat tricks for West Ham United?
   A. Les Ferdinand
   B. Teddy Sheringham
   C. Vic Watson

Here are the answers to the last set of questions.

A21. The Hammers' record victory in any competition was a whopping 10-0 in a League Cup match.

A22. This demolition job came against Bury, who seemingly have never recovered as they wallow in the lower leagues of English football.

A23. The game took place on 25th October 1983 in the 1983/84 season, although the Hammers couldn't convert this sort of form into lifting the trophy that season.

A24. West Ham's record league victory is 8-0.

A25. West Ham's record league victory was a crushing 8-0 victory in the old First Division on 19th October 1968 against Sunderland. They also recorded an 8-0 victory in the old Second Division on 8th March 1958 against Rotherham. Give yourself a bonus point if you knew that.

A26. The record victories came in the 1957/58 and 1968/69 seasons.

A27. The Irons' record defeat was a heavy 0-7 defeat in the old First Division.

A28. Sheffield Wednesday were responsible for West Ham's record defeat. The loss occurred on 28th November 1959.

A29. West Ham's record Premier League victory was a 6-0 win against Barnsley on 10th January 1998.

A30. All-time leading goal scorer Vic Watson also holds the record for most hat tricks scoring 13 hat tricks in his time at the club.

Now we move onto questions about the club's trophies.

31. How many times have West Ham United won the League?
    A. 0
    B. 1
    C. 2

32. How many times have West Ham United won the FA Cup?
    A. 2
    B. 3
    C. 4

33. How many times have they won the League Cup?
    A. 0
    B. 1
    C. 2

34. How many times have the club won a major European competition?
    A. 1
    B. 2
    C. 3

35. When did the club win their first FA Cup?
    A. 1964
    B. 1965
    C. 1966

36. Who did they beat in the final?
    A. Portsmouth

B. Peterborough United

C. Preston North End

37. When did the club last win the FA Cup?

    A. 1964

    B. 1975

    C. 1980

38. Who did they beat in the final?

    A. Arsenal

    B. Fulham

    C. Tottenham Hotspur

39. What was the score?

    A. 1-0

    B. 2-1

    C. 3-2

40. Who was the last captain to lift the FA Cup?

    A. Billy Bonds

    B. Alvin Martin

    C. Martin Peters

Here are the answers to the last block of questions.

A31. West Ham has never won the League. Although they have never been champions of the top division in England, West Ham has been Second Division Champions twice, winning the trophy in 1957/58 and in 1980/81.

A33. West Ham has won the FA Cup three times.

A33. West Ham has never won the League Cup but has been runners up twice.

A34. West Ham won the European Cup Winners Cup in 1965. The club won the Europa Conference League in 2023.

A35. The Hammers captured their first FA Cup on 2nd May 1964.

A36. West Ham were victorious on this occasion against Preston North End, winning a thrilling contest 3-2, coming from behind twice with goals from John Sissons, Geoff Hurst and Ronnie Boyce in the last minute, in front of 100,000 fans at Wembley. Bobby Moore was the captain on the day.

A37. West Ham last won the FA Cup in 1980.

A38. On 10th May 1980 West Ham was victorious against hot favourites Arsenal.

A39. The Hammers won an enthralling game 1-0 with the goal coming from a header by Trevor Brooking in the 13th minute.

A40. Billy Bonds was the captain who held the FA Cup aloft that glorious day in May.

I hope you're having fun and getting most of the answers right.

41. What is the record transfer fee paid?
   A. £31.2 million
   B. £41.2 million
   C. £51.2 million

42. Who was the record transfer fee paid for?
   A. Sebastien Haller
   B. Lucas Paqueta
   C. Kurt Zouma

43. What is the record transfer fee received?
   A. £85 million
   B. £95 million
   C. £105 million

44. Who was the record transfer fee received for?
   A. Craig Bellamy
   B. Dimitri Payet
   C. Declan Rice

45. Who has won the most international caps whilst a West Ham United player?
   A. James Collins
   B. David James
   C. Bobby Moore

46. Who has scored the most international goals whilst a West Ham United player?
   A. Jermain Defoe

B. Geoff Hurst

C. Teddy Sheringham

47. Who is the youngest player ever to represent the club?

    A. Neil Finn

    B. Mark Noble

    C. Reece Oxford

48. Who is the youngest ever goalscorer?

    A. Michael Carrick

    B. Joe Cole

    C. Jermain Defoe

49. Who is the oldest player ever to represent the club?

    A. Stuart Pearce

    B. Teddy Sheringham

    C. Nigel Winterburn

50. Who is West Ham United's oldest ever goal scorer?

    A. Brian Dear

    B. Teddy Sheringham

    C. Vic Watson

Here are the answers to the last set of questions.

A41. The most West Ham has ever paid for a single player is a reported £51.2 million.

A42. On 29th August 2022, West Ham paid Lyon £51.2 million for Lucas Paqueta.

A43. West Ham's record amount received for a player stands at £105 million.

A44. In July 2023, Arsenal paid West Ham £105 million for Declan Rice.

A45. England's most successful ever captain, Bobby Moore won all of his 108 England caps whilst in the claret and blue of West Ham.

A46. World Cup winner Geoff Hurst scored all 24 of his international goals whilst he was a West Ham player, including his famous hat trick in the World Cup Final in 1966.

A47. The youngest player ever to represent the club used to be Neil Finn, who played just one game for the club back in January 1996 at the tender age of just 17 years and 2 days. However, his record was beaten, on 2nd July 2015, when Reece Oxford made his debut in a Europa League game, aged just 16 years and 198 days. He made his Premier League debut a little over a month later on 9th August 2015, aged just 16 years and 235 days.

A48. Boy wonder (now retired of course) Joe Cole scored for West Ham against Birmingham City in the League Cup on 30th November 1999 aged just 18 years and 22 days.

A49. Evergreen Teddy Sheringham is the oldest player in Hammers history, playing in the Premier League at the ripe old age of 40 years and 272 days against Manchester City on 30th December 2006.

A50. West Ham's oldest ever player is also the club's oldest scorer. Teddy Sheringham scored on Boxing Day 2006 in the Premier League against Portsmouth aged 40 years and 268 days, breaking his own record in the process.

I hope you're learning some new facts about the Hammers.

51. Who was the first West Ham United player to play for England?
    A. George Moncur
    B. George Parris
    C. George Webb

52. Who is the club's longest serving manager of all time?
    A. Syd King
    B. Charlie Paynter
    C. Harry Redknapp

53. Who is the club's longest serving post-war manager?
    A. Ted Fenton
    B. Ron Greenwood
    C. John Lyall

54. What is the name of the West Ham United match day programme?
    A. Hammer Time
    B. We Are West Ham
    C. West Ham United

55. Who started the 2024/25 season as manager?
    A. Slaven Bilic
    B. Julen Lopetegui
    C. David Moyes

56. Which was a popular West Ham United fanzine?

A. Boleyn Bulletin
B. Green Street News
C. Knees Up Mother Brown

57. What motif is on the club crest?
    A. A castle and two crossed hammers
    B. A hammer and sickle
    C. Two crossed hammers

58. What is the club's motto?
    A. Arte et Labore
    B. Audere est Facere
    C. No motto

59. Who is considered as West Ham United's main rivals?
    A. Arsenal
    B. Charlton
    C. Millwall

60. What could be regarded as the club's most well-known song?
    A. How Much is that Doggy in the Window
    B. I'm Forever Blowing Bubbles
    C. Knees Up Mother Brown

Here are the answers to the last set of questions.

A51. George Webb was the first Hammer ever to represent England, scoring on his debut all the way back on 13th March 1911. He made just one more appearance, but sadly died of tuberculosis aged just 27. Incidentally, Webb scored on his Hammers debut too.

A52. Syd King was West Ham's first manager and also the longest serving. He was at the reins for 638 games for thirty years from 1902 to 1932. He later committed suicide.

A53. A faithful servant of the club for 34 years, John Lyall was manager for 15 of those years, from April 1974 until June 1989; making him the club's longest serving manager in the post-war era.

A54. The programme available to fans on match days is simply called West Ham United.

A55. Julen Lopetegui started the 2024/25 season as manager. He was appointed to the role in May 2024.

A56. Knees Up Mother Brown is probably the best known of the club's fanzines. It now has a very popular website with plenty of regularly updated online material.

A57. West Ham's crest has evolved a lot over the years, and it is now has a clean and modern design with two crossed hammers.

A58. West Ham do not in fact have an official motto, although the phrase "Onwards and Upwards" has been adopted by some fans in recent times.

A59. The Hammers' fiercest rivalry is with Millwall, and fans eagerly look forward to this match when the clubs are drawn together in the various cup competitions.

A60. No Hammers fan will get this one wrong. "I'm Forever Blowing Bubbles" is synonymous with West Ham United and is sung with pride by fans at every game, home and away.

Let's give you some easier questions.

61. What is the traditional colour of the home shirt?
    A. Cerise and Blue
    B. Claret and Blue
    C. Crimson and Blue

62. What is the traditional colour of the away shirt?
    A. Black
    B. Light Blue
    C. Red

63. Who is the current shirt sponsor?
    A. Alpari
    B. Betway
    C. SBOBET

64. Who was the first club sponsor?
    A. AVCO Trust
    B. Dagenham Motors
    C. Dr. Martens

65. Which of these have once sponsored the club?
    A. JobAbout
    B. JobServe
    C. JobShop

66. Who is currently the club chair?
    A. Vanessa Gold
    B. David Sullivan
    C. Both Gold & Sullivan

67. Who is currently the club's vice-chairman?
    A. Karren Brady
    B. Terence Brown
    C. Andy Mollett

68. Who was the club's first black player?
    A. Clyde Best
    B. John Charles
    C. Marc Vivien Foe

69. Where is West Ham's training ground?
    A. Carrington
    B. Chadwell Heath
    C. Epping Forest

70. Who was the supporters' player of the year – the
    Hammer of the Year - for 2024?
    A. James Ward-Prowse
    B. Jarrod Bowen
    C. Tomas Soucek

Here are the answers to the last set of questions.

A61. No excuses if you get this one wrong; of course they wear Claret and Blue.

A62. West Ham's away strip is usually of a light blue.

A63. The Hammers currently have a shirt sponsorship deal with online gaming platform Betway.

A64. The club's first ever shirt sponsor was AVCO Trust, who started sponsoring the club in 1983.

A65. Jobserve sponsored the club from 2003 to 2007.

A66. West Ham have David Sullivan and Vanessa Gold as joint chair. That's a better way than saying chairman and chairwoman apparently.

A67. Baroness Karren Brady is the club's vice-chairman, or vice-chairwoman if you prefer.

A68. John Charles became the first black player to represent the Hammers. Right back "Charlo" was born in Canning Town, and made his debut, aged 19, in May 1963. He went on to play 118 times for the club.

A69. The West Ham players put in the hours on the training ground based at Chadwell Heath in Essex.

A70. West Ham's supporters honoured Jarrod Bowen with the Hammer of the Year award for 2024. Well deserved it was too.

Right, on with the questions.

71. Who has made the most consecutive appearances for West Ham United?
    A. Joe Cockcroft
    B. Julian Dicks
    C. Shaka Hislop

72. How many times have West Ham won the FA Youth Cup?
    A. 2
    B. 3
    C. 4

73. Who started the 2023/24 season as West Ham's captain?
    A. Jarrod Bowen
    B. Aaron Creswell
    C. Kurt Zouma

74. How many West Ham players were in the 1966 World Cup winning England team?
    A. 1
    B. 2
    C. 3

75. Which hero scored two goals in the 1965 European Cup Winners Cup Final?
    A. Joe Kirkup
    B. Alan Sealey
    C. John Sissons

76. What position did the club finish at the end of the 2023/24 season?
    A. 9th
    B. 10th
    C. 11th

77. Which West Ham player retired through injury in 1996, only to play for Atletico Madrid a year later?
    A. Ricardo Carvalho
    B. Paulo Futre
    C. Diego Simeone

78. How many players passed through the club when Harry Redknapp was manager?
    A. 74
    B. 104
    C. 134

79. Who did Alvin Martin score a hat trick against in 1986 with each goal scored against a different goalkeeper?
    A. Middlesbrough
    B. Newcastle United
    C. Sunderland

80. Which of these manufacturers has not supplied kit to West Ham?
    A. Adidas
    B. Nike
    C. Umbro

Here are the answers to the last set of questions.

A71. Joe Cockcroft holds the record for most successive appearances, with 208 back in the 1930s. In today's era of squad rotation, it is unlikely this record will ever be beaten.

A72. West Ham have won the FA Youth Cup three times - in 1963, 1981 and 1999.

A73. Kurt Zouma started the 2023/24 season as club captain.

A74. The famous trio of Bobby Moore, Martin Peters and Geoff Hurst were the three West Ham players in the England side.

A75. Alan Sealey was the hero as West Ham beat TSV 1860 Munich in the 1965 European Cup Winners Cup Final at Wembley, scoring both goals in a 2-0 victory. All eleven starting players were English. How times have changed!

A76. West Ham finished the 2023/24 season in 9th position.

A77. Paulo Futre retired through injury in 1996, and West Ham fans were surprised to see him playing again in Spain a year later. Anyone got the number for his doctor?

A78. An incredible 134 players passed through the club while wheeler dealer Redknapp was manager between August 1994 and May 2001.

A79. On 21st April 1986 Alvin Martin scored a hat trick in an 8-1 victory over Newcastle United in a top flight match. Incredibly, each of his goals was scored against a different goalkeeper. Unfortunately for Newcastle, injuries to their first and then replacement goalkeepers meant West Ham faced three keepers: Martin Thomas, Chris Hedworth and finally England striker, Peter Beardsley.

A80. Nike has never supplied kit to West Ham, whereas Adidas and Umbro, amongst others, have.

We are approaching the end; I hope you're doing well.

81. Who has won the Hammer of the Year award the most times?
    A. Trevor Brooking
    B. Julian Dicks
    C. Alvin Martin

82. Who has won the Hammer of the Year award three times in a row?
    A. Paolo Di Canio
    B. Kevin Nolan
    C. Scott Parker

83. What is the club's official twitter account?
    A. @WestHam
    B. @WestHamUnited
    C. @WHUFC

84. What nationality is Paolo Di Canio?
    A. Brazilian
    B. Italian
    C. Portuguese

85. What is West Ham's best-placed finish ever?
    A. 3rd
    B. 5th
    C. 7th

86. What is West Ham's best-placed finish in the Premier League era?
    A. 5th

B. 6th

C. 7th

87. What shirt number does Aaron Cresswell wear?

A. 3

B. 13

C. 23

88. What is West Ham's record number of home wins in a row?

A. 14

B. 15

C. 16

89. Who was West Ham's first ever foreign manager?

A. Paolo Di Canio

B. Avram Grant

C. Gianfranco Zola

90. Who was the first player from outside of Europe to captain West Ham United?

A. Javier Mascherano

B. Lucas Neill

C. Mark Vivien Foe

Here are the answers to the last block of questions.

A81. Trevor Brooking won the Hammer of the Year award five times. It is an incredible achievement.

A82. Tireless midfielder Scott Parker won the Hammer of the Year award three years running, from 2009 to 2011.

A83. @WestHam is the club's official twitter account. It tweets multiple times daily and it has nearly three million followers.

A84. Di Canio was born in Rome, Italy.

A85. West Ham's best ever finish was 3rd, in the 1985/86 season. The club finished on 84 points, just 4 points behind the champions Liverpool. The season was one of free-flowing attacking fluidity led by a double headed strike force of Frank McAvennie and Tony Cottee who rattled in 26 and 20 league goals respectively. Unfortunately, there was no European football the following season due to the UEFA ban on English clubs in the wake of the Heysel disaster when 39 spectators died as a result of rioting by Liverpool fans.

A86. West Ham's best finish in the Premier League era is an impressive 5th place, back in the 1998/99 season.

A87. Aaron Cresswell wears the number 3 shirt.

A88. West Ham won 16 home games in a row between August 1980 and March 1981.

A89. Zola became the first ever foreign manager of the club when he was appointed on 15th September 2008.

A90. Australian defender Lucas Neill became West Ham's first non-European captain in 2007, and he held the position for two years.

Right, here we go. We are into the final straight.

91. Who currently supplies kit to the first team?
    A. Adidas
    B. Macron
    C. Umbro

92. Where was Dutch footballer Marco Boogers rumoured to be sleeping, after going AWOL when playing for West Ham United?
    A. In a caravan
    B. In a car park
    C. In a cave

93. Which Hollywood actor starred in the film 'Green Street' about a firm of West Ham supporting football hooligans?
    A. Ashton Kutcher
    B. Tobey Maguire
    C. Elijah Wood

94. Which World Cup Golden Boot winner only managed three goals in a disappointing spell with West Ham United?
    A. Luis Boa Morte
    B. Diego Poyet
    C. Davor Suker

95. Which of these celebrities is a West Ham United fan?
    A. Dennis Waterman
    B. Roger Waters

C. Ray Winstone

96. Where was the 2023 UEFA Europa Conference League final held?
    A. Paris
    B. Porto
    C. Prague

97. Who did West Ham beat in the 2023 UEFA Europa Conference League final?
    A. AZ Alkmaar
    B. Fiorentina
    C. Gent

98. Who scored the winning goal in the 2023 UEFA Europa Conference League final?
    A. Said Benrahma
    B. Jarrod Bowen
    C. Tomáš Souček

99. Who is the only player in the Official West Ham United Dream Team not from the United Kingdom?
    A. Paolo Di Canio
    B. Shaka Hislop
    C. Carlos Tevez

100. What is the club's official website address?
    A. hammers.com
    B. westham.co.uk
    C. whufc.com

101. Here we go with the last question. Who is honoured with a statue near the ground?
   A. Geoff Hurst
   B. Bobby Moore
   C. Martin Peters

Here are the answers to the final set of questions.

A91. Umbro currently produce all of the Hammers' official kits, from first team to youth level, as well as training products and leisure wear for players and fans.

A92. The Sun newspaper published a story claiming that Marco Boogers was convalescing in a caravan after being sent off playing for the Hammers in only his second game for the club in August 1995. In total, Boogers managed just four substitute appearances totalling 44 minutes in his time at the club.

A93. From the fires of Mordor to an equally hostile environment, Elijah Wood starred in the film Green Street. Violence and questionable accents aplenty.

A94. Davor Suker top scored at the 1998 World Cup, and managed more goals at that tournament that he did in a whole season at Upton Park.

A95. Famous East Ender turned Hollywood actor Ray Winstone is one of West Ham's most famous fans, with Russell Brand a close second.

A96. The 2023 UEFA Europa Conference League final was held on 7th June 2023 in Prague. What a night, that will live long in the memory.

A97. West Ham beat Fiorentina of Italy 2-1 in the Final.

A98. Jarrod Bowen scored the winner in the 90th minute. What a goal it was too.

A99. The mercurial Italian Paolo Di Canio is the only player to make the 2003 Official West Ham United Dream Team who hails from outside the United Kingdom.

A100. whufc.com is the official website address.

A101. All three West Ham legends are in a statue near the ground, as is Ray Wilson. It is a bronze statue in Barking Road, opposite The Boleyn Tavern which depicts a famous victory scene after the 1966 World Cup Final with Moore holding the Jules Rimet World Cup trophy aloft.

That's it. That's a great question to finish with. I hope you enjoyed this book, and I hope you got most of the answers right. I also hope you learnt a few new things about the club.

support@glowwormpress.com is the email address if you saw anything wrong, or you have any comments or suggestions.

Thanks for reading, and if you did enjoy the book, would you please leave a positive review on Amazon.

COYI.